ghost on 3rd

Also by Jim Reese

These Trespasses, The Backwaters Press, 2005, 2006

Chapbooks

The Jive, Morpo Press, 2004
Wedding Cake and Funeral Ham, Grizzly Press, 2002

ghost on 3rd

Jim Reese

 Books™

The New York Quarterly Foundation, Inc.
New York, New York

NYQ Books™ is an imprint of The New York Quarterly Foundation, Inc.

The New York Quarterly Foundation, Inc.
P. O. Box 2015
Old Chelsea Station
New York, NY 10113

www.nyqbooks.org

Copyright © 2010 by Jim Reese

All rights reserved. No part of this book may be used or reproduced in any manner whatsoever without written permission of the author. This book is a work of fiction. Any references to historical events, real people or real locales are used fictitiously. Other names, characters, places, and incidents are products of the author's imagination, and any resemblance to actual events or locales or persons, living or dead, is entirely coincidental.

First Edition

Set in New Baskerville
Cover font Bauer Bodoni

Layout and Design by Raymond P. Hammond

Cover Illustration:
"Two Heads in Cloudscape," 2001, by Bret Gottschall | www.gotty.com

Cover design by Natalie Sousa

Library of Congress Control Number: 2009939408

ISBN: 978-1-935520-17-7

ghost on 3rd

Acknowledgments

Grateful acknowledgments to the editors of the following journals in which these poems, sometimes in early versions, first appeared or are forthcoming: "Vernon is Taking the Dirty Dog Home," *4 P. M. Count*; "The Day Before You Broke Your Arm on the Monkey Bars," "The Keeper of All Things Necessary and Whole," *Caduceus*; "Running with Wine," *Cairn*; "Hunting for Crawlers," "A Pony for Paige," *Connecticut Review*; "It's not what you know, it's who you know," "Irene Pop 470 00," "Fordyce, Population 190+1," *Connecticut River Review*; "Memorial Day 2007, Hartington, Nebraska," "Waiting for the Greatest Show on Earth to Start," *Expressions*; "Playing with Balloons, Needles and Peas," and "As Seen on TV," *Louisiana Literature Review*; "Habit," *Mid-America Poetry Review*; "A Bag of Apples," *Nebraska Life*; "The Sandwich Shop," "This Havelock," "Would you mind reading this new poem of mine?" *New York Quarterly*; "Makes for 4 Persons," "Diving in the Bathtub," "This is Nebraska," "It's My Party and I'll Cry if I Want To," "How Do You Like My M's," "The Woman Who Wishes to Remain Anonymous," "His Secret Stash," *Paterson Literary Review*; "Mothers—A Toast," "What They Do Not Tell Us," *Poetry East*; "Coming to Grips," "This Hunger," "At Two Years," *Prairie Schooner* by permission of the University of Nebraska Press; "Missing," "The Keeper of All Things Necessary and Whole," "The Grass Alley," *South Dakota Review*; "Fry Cook, Stockade Bar and Grill," and "The Pecker," *Talking River Review*. Acknowledgment is also given to the editors of these broadsides and anthologies: "Triple Dog Dares," Poster Design by Young Ae Kim for the P3 Invitational Exhibition of paired poems and artwork—Washington Pavilion of Arts and Science, Sioux Falls, SD, 2008; "My Five-Year-Old Daughter Questions Death and Spatulas," plus eleven previously published poems, *South Dakota Poetry Reader*, Center for Western Studies; "So, This is Nebraska," *Red Thread Gold Thread: The Poet's Voice*, 2009 ed. Alan Cohen; and *Power of Poetry Press*, Hockin' County, Ohio.

Thanks to Raymond Hammond and the fine staff at the *New York Quarterly* for believing in my work.

For Willow, Paige and Linda

*and for Cecil Brandenburg
and Bill Kloefkorn,
my favorite storytellers.*

Contents

This Havelock /13
So, This is Nebraska /14
Fordyce Population 190+1 /16
What They Do Not Tell Us /17
As Seen on TV /18
The Woman Who Wishes to Remain Anonymous Bakes a Cherry Pie /20
A Bag of Apples /21
Coming to Grips /22
At Three Years My Daughter Recites Her First Poem /24
This Hunger /25
Running with Wine /26
At Two Years /27
Sandwich Shop—Lincoln, NE 2006 /28
Fry Cook, Stockade Bar and Grill, Millard, Nebraska, 1985 /29
South Dakota Bumper Stickers /30
The Names People Give Us /33
Playing with Balloons, Needles and Peas /34
It's not what you know, it's who you know. /36
Keep it Between the Ditches /37
The Keeper of All Things Whole and Necessary /38
Memorial Day 2007, Hartington, Nebraska /40
God Bless America /41
Coming Soon: Live Bait and Tackle /42
How do you like my M's? /43
Would you mind reading this new poem? /44
Triple Dog Dares /45
Irene Pop. 470 00 /46
Diving in the Bathtub /47
ThIS IS A HOLDUp /48
Ghost on 3rd /50

The Grass Alley /52
It's My Birthday /53
A Pony for Paige /54
Waking to SQ /56
Jesus Christ Pose /61
I was at San Quentin and All I Got was This Lousy T-shirt /62
In a Stall in a College John /64
MISSING /66
Habit /68
Vernon is Taking the Dirty Dog Home /69
The Metal Detector /70
Another Poem about the Rain /72
The Pecker /73
His Secret Stash /74
Makes for 4 Persons /76
Poetry Reading—Tonite /78
Sneaker /80
The Day Before You Broke Your Wrist on the Monkey Bars /81
My Five Year Old Daughter Questions Death and Spatulas /82
Mothers—*A Toast* /83

ghost on 3rd

This Havelock

Possessive Dandelions. Snot-nosed kids blowin' snowball-seeds into headwind. Then I come upon three plumber cracks bending over a '77 Vega, Old Milwaukee in each right hand, pocket-pool with each left. Fremont Street is full blown with Harleys and homebrew, glass packs and malnourished mufflers. People driving. People bath-tub speeding. *Say, Sugar, you got somewhere to go or are you just going?* It's tube-tops and flip-flops, sidewalk stubbed toes—bare knuckle, and third-shift swing—Arnold's Bar for orange breakfast beers, rocket fuel gin, the finger stir and Family Feud. Tobacco Shack porn and Misty's blackened prime—California Lunch Room brown bags and Bob's shuffle board. It's the Isles for hip-show tattoos and a Leaning Tower pie. It's rode hard and put away thirsty—4 1/2 amps on a hump day—feeling a need for a need. I have to leave you, Havelock—this is my last stop—stay here much longer, I won't make it to the week's end.

So, This Is Nebraska

> *—for the guy in NYC who asked me, "Nebraska? Do you guys still ride around in a horse and buggy there?"*

Pa said Bobby and me could go fishing down at Snake Creek
just as soon as we graft this here calf
and finish stacking round bales
up in the loft of the barn.

Pa said we could go play with the Indians down the road, too,
but ma won't let us
on account of Man Sits In Tree is still fixin'
to finish skinning a buffalo and make hisself
a new teepee today.

So today, like most days,
we'll likely watch them big airplanes blow by overhead.
I wish people would just stop
every now and again for a visit.

I was fixin' to go walk up the hill
and pick some cherries,
but Bobby got a tick up in his britches—
stuck to his nutsack.
Ma said maybe he was up there
doing more than picking cherries
and won't let none of us go up the hill no more.
Ma predicts the Pony Express is due to arrive this week.
Maybe Bobby and I can go sit at the end of the lane
and wait for him and his horse.
It's really nifty to see him race by
and toss Bobby
our stack of mail. And sometimes even,
there's a Sears Roebuck catalog with girly pictures
for us to look at in the outhouse.

And maybe, just maybe, we could take the buggy to town,
get us some candy—stare at all them city folk
with their fancy hats and boots.
And maybe, just maybe, we could
take on a picture show while Pa
does his business around town.
Maybe Loretta Swinson will be there in town, too.
Yessum, yessum, I do believe she's true.

Fordyce Population 190+1

It's ten-thirty in the morning
and I walk next door to The Station to grab
a candy bar and pop.
Two early-bird elbow-benders are belly-up
to the bar drinking whiskey presses.

I pay, and on my way out I
see the new sign hanging on the wall—

>*Fordyce, Nebraska*
Too Small For a Town Drunk
>*So We Take Turns*

I tell the mechanic next door
I like the new sign they put up
in the bar.

Shit, he says.
That's no joke.

What They Do Not Tell Us

> *...sharing every cold*
> *observing agonies*
> *they cannot tell at home...*
> —Nancy Henry

It bothers me
when I see my wife get off
from a twelve-hour shift,
come home and lie lifeless on the couch.
Losing herself in the television.
Sometimes curling up in a ball.

When I ask her how work was,
she says, *We got our asses*
handed to us. People died.
Same old shit.

What I'm learning is,
there is nothing I can say or do.

I will never know what it's like to
watch a twenty-two-week-old baby hang on
for three more months.

Will never know what it's like
to scrape dead flesh from burnt living bodies.

Will never know what it's like to
rise at five a.m. and stay on my feet until seven p.m.
without much break, without lunch,
and, god willing, without error.

Will never know what it feels like to
turn code, stabilize, and then realize
I've forgotten one easy last step.

Will never know the satisfaction of flying to Kentucky
or Idaho, from Nebraska—in a twin prop—
to bring a baby back to life.

Will never know what it's like,
except this:
People died. Same old shit.

As Seen on TV

The giant in first class is on flight 455 to Newark.
The guy next to me wonders if he's Andre the Giant.
No. He's dead, the flight attendant says.
*They only live so long because they grow so fast. Bone
degeneration.*
She looks at me and I say, *I'll have a giant vodka and orange juice.*
I pick up the Sky Mall catalog and start to leaf through.

A famous poet has said there are fifty of us on any given day
in the air flying to and from readings. Today, only one
poet on the same plane as a giant wrestler—I betcha.
I'm tempted to concoct some sort of spit wad
or non-identifiable object to throw at the back of the big guy's head,
but the blue ruckus-reducing partition that divides us makes that
nearly impossible.

I don't want to piss him off. Just mess with him a little—get his attention,
so I can ask him all those important questions.
How big were your feet when you were born?
How many boxes of macaroni and cheese
can you eat before you come up for air?
How fast could you kick this guy's ass next to me
for blowing that spit wad at the back of your head?
He'd have everyone's attention, hunkered over in coach—
each hand bigger than a headrest, eye-balling us.

Until I can make that happen, I have settled for this catalog—the
indoor dog restroom and its antimicrobial porous turf—
ideal for high-rise dwellings.
Think gravity-defying boots and their patented T-spring system. An exhilarating
low impact bounce—perfect for keeping tabs on the giant
in your neighborhood.
Interested in firm, sexy buns in two weeks? I am.
The Shape and Form thingamajigger

comes with unique toning pads that lift while you sit.
When sporting your lifter why not wear your Flair Hair Visor.
A built-in do and hat. And don't forget that portable
10" x 12" personal microwave—perfect for nuking
your soup on the run.

Upon arriving in Newark I move out of turn to first class—to get one last look at the giant.
He reaches into an overhead compartment to retrieve his camouflage
carry-on case. The guy behind him ducks and I eagerly reach up to assist him
so he doesn't knock his squirmy neighbor in the head.
I smile up to him—he kinda smiles a friendly
giant smirk back.

The Woman Who Wishes to Remain Anonymous Bakes a Cherry Pie

My father-in-law and I are eating dinner with the woman who wishes
to remain anonymous—Swedish meatballs, potatoes, corn and bread.

You won't believe this, the anonymous woman says.
But I found a container of cherries that I froze in 1978.
They still looked good. So I made a pie out of them.

We've been eating it and haven't got sick yet, my father-in-law says.
That's the gospel truth.

There wasn't a lot of freezer burn on them? I ask.

Some, but not that much. And she shows me the container
the cherries were in. *And you cannot write about this or tell anyone*
who I am, until you try a piece for yourself. That's the deal.

Bring it on.

The woman who wishes to remain anonymous
reaches into the freezer, because she has already frozen the pie;
she doesn't want the leftovers to go to waste.
She thaws two pieces in the microwave.

My father-in-law cuts a piece and eats.

Are you sure it didn't say 1998? I ask.

The woman smiles.

I dig in.

A Bag of Apples

I grab a chair and scoot up to the kitchen table
where my father-in-law is playing solitaire.
His calloused hands thumb the cards
over and over until the deck is done.
This round he wins.
He scoops, shuffles and wraps a rubber band
around the deck of cards
and puts them into
the breast pocket of his coveralls.

He reaches for two apples from a bowl on the table.
Places one in front of me
and the other he takes a bite of.

You won't believe this, he says.
*I was out at the dump today
and saw this perfectly good bag of apples
just sitting there.*

I look at him. He is looking
at me. When he grins,
I bite into my apple.

Coming to Grips

We are grilling out at a friend's house.
Drinking a little beer, eating chips, hotdogs, hamburgers—
someone made artichoke dip.

You are running in the backyard,
climbing on patio furniture,
chasing the dog.

Up and down and running.
Up and down and running.
Chasing the dog.

The other kids are playing
football.
Babies, nursing.

Your mother is inside.
I can see her
from where I'm sitting.

And I catch a glimpse of you
out of the corner of my eye.
You have climbed too high

on one of the plastic patio chairs,
lost your balance.
And in one motion

I am up,
arms outstretched,
reaching, reaching.

I catch your shoulders
inches before
your head hits the cement.
You laugh.
You don't know how close
you came.

Your mother doesn't see any of this.
Some of the other parents
sigh.
No one says anything.
I am holding on to you,
tight.

We wave up to mom
in the window.
She waves back.

You say, *Wee!*
Everyone continues to play.
Someone scores a touchdown.

At Three Years My Daughter Recites Her First Poem

Dad. Look!
I'm a stinky monkey
hanging on the doorknob
like a fart.

This Hunger

Ceiling fans and flashlights.
Shoestrings and electric cords.
Mashed green beans and carrots.
Her best friends, the left and right breast.

Before she was one
I would count the scoops of food,
tally them up and tell her.
Four, let's eat some more.
Eight and donate to the stomach.
14 ½ ounces today.

And now, at two years,
it's *daddy…*

I like pizza.
I like pizza.
I like pizza.
I like pizza.

I like.   I like puddin.
I like puddinngg.

I like meat.
I like applesas.
I like.
I like pizza.

This hunger.
This hunger
growing.

Running with Wine

This is what I remember:
and I wish you would go away.
Walking down 60th Street with

Todd Shonkwieler, smoking Camels.
Going
nowhere.

I remember you passing us on the sidewalk,
darting across the street
toward Elmwood Park

between dimly lit street lights—
your shadow,
running.

And then screech! Brakes. Thud.
Bottle breaking. Exhaust.
You lying motionless on the street—tires spinning away.

One of us ran to call for help.
Both of us standing over you soon enough, checking your pulse,
staring at your face—beautiful, pale.

Sirens ringing. Cops showing up.
One of us pointing out the broken wine bottle
you'd been carrying.
Maybe she's drunk, one of us said.
The police officer kneeling down to inspect the bag
the bottle was in.

No. It's corked,
the officer said slowly.
I believe she had plans for this evening.

At Two Years

My daughter and I have concluded the following.

Yes, she will be a professional bullfighter.
Yes, she will be a professional hopper.
Yes, she will be a helicopter.
I can be a helicopter, I can.
Yes, she may be the pilot of a helicopter, too.

She will be a professional wrestler,
A professional swimmer and diver.
I can jump off the high board. I can.

A professional ballerina and
Blue-gill catcher.

Yes. Yes. Yes.

Sandwich Shop—Lincoln, NE 2006

I'm eating a triple Italian melt
with hot peppers and au jus
when Jake sits down in his chair
positioned in front of CNN.

You know back in Chicago,
in the 80's we had a gas shortage.
It was rationed—you could only get $10 worth.
That didn't get you far in Chicago—prices over $2.00
a gallon. You know what the problem is is
all those people driving SUV's in California.
I bet that guy drives an SUV.

The phone rings.
Jake gets up and answers—I listen.

Listen, he says,
my hands are tied here. There's nothing I can do.
I gave the guy your number, that's all I can do.
He listens some more. I listen.
Yeah, you know, there's nothing I can do.
There's nothing more I can do for you. I told him you called here
yesterday. That's it. There's nothing I can do.

Jake hangs up the phone.
Except break your fucking head.
And sits back down to watch some more CNN.

How's the sandwich? he asks.
Perfect, I tell him.

Fry Cook, Stockade Bar and Grill, Millard, Nebraska, 1985

Fourteen years old on a four-to-nine o'clock work permit making three dollars and fifteen cents an hour scrubbing pots and pans at the Stockade Bar and Grill—*You're not finished yet*—peeling four five gallon buckets of Idaho potatoes until one o'clock in the morning. Hands scalded a permanent red from stacking hot plates, griddle platters, breaking water glasses—*That's coming out of your paycheck, friend. You know how much each of those glasses costs me? Not another snot-nosed pecker that can't hold on to a sip cup!* Black shoes standing on a black rubber mat, smell of greasy fried chicken and Salisbury steak—brown gravy on a mandatory white-collared dress shirt—*Order up! Order up! Order up! Food's ice cold.* Brown door smacking me in the head, dropping bus carts in the entryway exit. *God damn, boy, you know how to fry a burger? Maybe you won't break so much shit back here. Come over and hold this. When those burgers start bleeding, flip 'em over, and when that side is bleeding smack and squish it down like so. Give me your forearm. Feel this here, here and here—that's rare, medium and done. Now watch that rib eye. He wants it black and blue.*

South Dakota Bumper Stickers

Have You Hugged Your Hog Today?

    I'M RETIRED
    Gone Fishin'

        GET OFF YOUR PHONE AND DRIVE

    EAT BEEF
The West Wasn't Won On Salad

      Horn Not Working
      Watch For Finger

        Working for an Idiot Free America

You are in INDIAN COUNTRY

      REPUBLICAN WOMEN are the life of the party

        GUN CONTROL
        Means Using Both Hands

This Year I Got a New Gun
For My Wife. Good Trade Don't Ya' Think?

      Where the Heck is
      WALL DRUG

        IF IT FLYS IT DIES

I remember Korea

DON'T LAUGH MISTER. YOUR DAUGHTER COULD BE ON BOARD!

Retired HOOTERS GIRL

Ted Nugent
Bow Hunters—**A**gainst—**D**rugs

STURGIS Ride To Live

I LOVE MY WIFE

You Just Got Passed by a Girl   (same car)   Bite Me

(same car) If You Are Going to Ride My Ass At Least Pull My Hair

Don't Mess with My Country

BAD ASS TOYZ
AREN'T JUST FOR BOYZ

My Drinking Team Has
A Demo Problem

Siouxland Eye Bank
Please Donate

My Other Auto Is a .45

Next time you are perfect try walking on water.

Charlton Hesston is MY PRESIDENT

Cowboy UP

You Can Have My Book When You Pry It from My Cold Dead Hands

My Other Car is a BROOM
I'd Rather Be at a Neil Diamond Concert

SUPPORT OUR TROOPS

BRING THEM HOME

        HALF MY HEART
         IS IN Iraq

Sure You Can Trust the Government
Just Ask an Indian

                              I know Jack Shit

        BOYCOTT Veal

It's Bush's Fault

                    Shut the Duck Up!!!

The Names People Give Us

Do they still call you Bucket Calf?
Cactus
Captain Nervous
Jimmy Nipples
Boy, they really broke the mold when they created you.
Kid
Lunker
Whiskey Boy
Dr. Paddlefish
That's our C Man.
Swimmer
Doc
Professor
Our Poet
Shamooker
Stump Trainer
That's my boy!
This is my husband Jim.
Daddy!

Playing with Balloons, Needles and Peas

A woman sitting across from me
in the emergency room is
losing it

into a small gray tub while talking
on her cell phone. I am
not losing it yet,

nor is my daughter, Willow, who
is here to lose the pea
stuck deeply

up into her nasal cavity. Nor is my wife,
who would be here on duty
if this weren't

> *Inflate a balloon and tie it off. Let a little air out before tying it completely. This way it will be easier to pop the balloon without breaking it. The balloon should not be longer than the needle.*

her night off. My daughter sneezes,
but no pea. She continues
to throw playing cards

> *Dip the entire needle or sharp skewer in some sort of cooking oil.*

on the cold ceramic tile. A woman in white scrubs
comes to take us in.
The doctor laughs,

> *In a gentle manner—insert the needle into the nipple end of the balloon.*

asks my wife, *Isn't this your night off?*
He goes in with an inflatable needle,
a device that looks

> *Continue pushing, twisting and turning the needle or skewer until you puncture the opposite side of the balloon (near the tied end).*

like a needle, but once inserted
and is past the intruder,
the tip expands.

> *Continue to pull the needle out near the tied end—the balloon will slowly lose air.*

The doctor's hands move precisely
and slowly; the pea, still green
and solid,

> *Once the needle is free, jab the balloon.*

is freed.

> *The balloon will pop.*

It's not what you know, it's who you know.

Your voice rattling in my head again,
waking me from my slumber.
These nights I come to in a hot sweat.

This hellish nightmare—back in the warehouse
maintaining the Optical Character Reader
or even worse—sorting endless flats,
smothered by meter machines and INS green cards
wishing I was the guy running the OCR.

You Bosslady with your thick eyeliner and glops of makeup—
your high heels that are two sizes too small,
hobbling out on the floor and barking out orders.
These days Happy Hour can't come fast enough.

My coworker with his hands on Megan's ass and tits,
Sharon in the break room with a black eye.
The floor manager scooting off for beers for lunch,
leaving his dope in the delivery van.

How we survived with our BS degrees in English
and our $6.00 an hour still haunts me.
Our plasma donations and our overnight experimental
paid laboratory stays—writing loaded checks
and Fast Bucks until payday
when we start the cycle all over again.

I saw you the other day Bosslady on a billboard
advertising your top-dollar earnings.
It's not what you know, it's who you know.
Isn't that what you always told us?
Isn't that what you're trying to sell us now?

Keep it Between the Ditches

Doon Doon Doom Doom
Doon Doon Doom Doom
chugging—black cloud coughing out of erect steel pipe;
riding the shoulder of Highway 81.
13 County farmers with their here I am orange Allis Chalmers,
International Reds, M's and Johnny Poppin' Deere's—onward.
2nd Annual WNAX Tri-State Old Iron Two-Day Tractor Ride.
Men finger-waving. Men gazing off to the right,
checking their neighbors' fields.

The Keeper of All Things Whole and Necessary

Puts leftover food in little plastic
baby food containers and yogurt cups
she has hoarded. Will leave
half a chicken wing
for someone else to eat.
Wraps up and refrigerates
one slice of bacon.
Puts lemon juice on half an apple
so it won't turn brown.
Washes and packrats
straws with holes and plastic silverware
with broken tines.
Has a drawer full of mustard,
barbeque and soy sauce packages
from take-out restaurants
from out of town.
Has personalized greeting cards
that she will white-out and reuse.

Cuts coupons (sometimes expired). Cuts up
and collects newspaper articles
if she knows someone in the article or
knows someone who knows the person
in the article.
Gives me play-by-plays of garage sales
and auctions.
Saves fresh scraps for stray cats—bones
for the dogs. Saves for Jesus
and saves for you.
Picks green tomatoes before the first winter freeze.
Wraps them in tissue paper—serves them for
Thanksgiving dinner.
Balances soap dispensers
upside-down like others do with

ketchup bottles, and eventually
combines them in one bottle.
Has a room full of old jeans
in case her husband's overalls
need patching or her son-in-law's
crotch blows out.

Makes pie crust from hog lard.
(The only way to make pie crust).
Has full canning jars from the 80's.
Has unidentifiable things older than dirt
in her deep freeze.

Once I saw her pull a tarp
for a pick-up bed out
from underneath her dresser.
I've been holding on to this,
I don't know how long.

If you need something—
a blow torch,
nunchucks, twist-ties,
marbles, propane, a chandelier,
suspenders, goat cheese, a curtain rod,
spare tire, a putter, basin wrench, bell bottoms, a bowling ball—
anything;
she's your woman.

Memorial Day 2007, Hartington, Nebraska

I see Vernie walking by the courthouse,
stopping every so often to glance up as American flags
reach from the sky down to the sidewalk.

You know, he tells me, *some of us veterans sat in on holy hours
today. Bell on the church kept going and going.
There are a lot of us from Hartington.*

*Bong, Bong, Bong. Church bell wouldn't stop.
How's a guy supposed to nap through all that racket?*

God Bless America

We are losing a war overseas and
everyone is drinking.

    Rat a TAT TAT

I am the Kleenex
your mother lined her glass
of sweet tea with
to absorb the perspiration
of this Fourth of July heat.

    President Bush's ratings are the lowest since Nixon.

The party is dandy, your mother kept repeating—
and *God bless America,*
as streamers of light sprayed the sky—
pyrotechnics galore,
her fist clenched around me.

    There are over 4,000 Americans dead.

        BOOM!

Here I am, wadded up tight—
little balls of paper,
dead in the fishnet cup holder
of this folding lounger
that will be packed away
until next year's independence celebration.

Coming Soon: Live Bait and Tackle

says a sign on the mini-fridge
awaiting nightcrawlers.
The walls shine with new chartreuse jigs, buzz-bait lures
and spinners. We are on the verge of catching crappie—
cabin-fever itch—gotta get out of town.
The ATM requires a $2.00 Transaction Fee.
Do You Want to Continue?
Do you have a choice?

Throw your 35 cents in the blue bowl
next to the coffee maker. A lineman walks by you
decked out in Carhartt coverall and a stocking cap.
Would it hurt to wear a tie to work? he jokes with you.
The gossip shop in the corner nurses Folgers,
drink, smoke, drink, smoke.

See Michael Landon on the television above the shotgun shells
and chew. Add some Sweet and Low.
I had to change the channel—watching Little House, now. The clerk says.
I can't stand to watch the news. We all know what's going on.
Notice that the Bud Light tallboys are already on ice
by the cash register.
Yeah, you got hope in one hand and shit in the other
and see which is the first to get full.
Try to laugh and leave.

How do you like my M's?

My wife asks.
They are supposed to be birds.
How about my purple horse?

It's bedtime for Willow, November 1.
We are grilling
and drinking day-old Vampire wine.

Chalk on the bricks.
A game of tic-tac-toe—no winner, no loser.
Sunshine, XXOOXO,
and fish.

The sidewalk art
glows with glee.
My daughter's sand box toys

are strewn across the yard.
It's nine o' clock and, for two more hours,
if Willow doesn't wake,

this time is ours.
The cool buzz of the baby monitor,
the cheesy brats bursting on the grill,
the gurgle and kiss.

Would you mind reading this new poem?

How long is it?

I just want your honest feedback.

Every time I tell you what I think you get all pissed off.

You're exaggerating.

Uh-huh. You really want me to tell you what I think?

Please. Usually when you don't like it,
it gets published.

Isn't that nice. Stir the sauce, it's starting to burn.

What?

In front of you—the sauce. And don't let the noodles boil too long.

What about this line...Free those breasts
and their veiny road maps....

Stop. I hate when you read it to me out loud. Just give me the damn thing.

Not if you're going to get all pissy about it.

Fine.

Great. The noodles are all soggy.

I told you.

Yes you did.

Triple Dog Dares

*I know a woman who collects stuffed black crows—
and I know why.*

When I was a teenager, living on Chandler Street, dodging traffic—sess-sliding with my homemade Hosoi-nose Gonzales-back skateboard—my father the actuary stopped me when I finally dragged home, said, *Death comes in* **threes.** We talked mortality. Risk. Losing a friend. *Threes. That's always been my experience.* I'd like to tell you I slowed down after that talk. It only got worse. I am obsessed with the number **three**. *Threes.* **Three** times I check my wallet because, once, my card was stolen—

gone. In front of my very eyes. Right now in my town, **three hearses**—body bags, polished shoes and impending grief. **Three** times I speak to myself until I realize you are staring. Look closer now and I'll try and quit—just **tap tap tap** until the voices, sometimes one sometimes two…I know everything, right now, might be better than fine. It could all go to hell in a basket of **three hand-me-downs**—smash, illness and demise. Can you see the itch? Twitch? **Tic toc…Tic?**

Don't look in my medicine cabinet. Don't read the post-it notes behind its mirror. **3:33** I wait by the nearest clock—**wish** and **skin** and **bone**. But also, there are three people I come home to in this house—luv and kin. Three of my favorite words—***sin*, *win*** and ***voodoo*. 321 21 1 1 12 123** Why? I have tasted my karma and **triple dog dares**—this I am sure of. I'm still walking from these tricks—unscathed.

Irene
Pop. 470 00

When I push through town
I notice the double-zeros someone has added
to your green census sign—
470 00.

Then I imagine them—the young couple,
just graduated from high school—the Indian summer
turning for worse.
Screw it, he says. Throws the spray paint
they used to decorate the sign with in the ditch—grabs her right hand
with his left, puts his other on the small
of her back—dip—dark, dirty kiss.
Let's blow this one horse.
She smiles, and tells him,
I'll go anywhere you want.

They jump in his rickety '79 Bonneville,
hit the corner store for fuel—
find some friends
on the board-bridge outatown who've bought beer.
They get out of the car for one last dance.
They laugh to themselves and gulp—
laugh, gulp, kiss—throw their empties
on gravel.

What's your hurry? one of the local girls says.
You are going to swallow each other's tongues.
That's when they know it's time.
Without another word, they reach for more drinks and
head back to his car where they jump in.
He grabs the elastic bungee cord—hooks it
behind her to the passenger door
and stretches it across to his door handle.
He revs the thing up—
stands on the gas.

Diving in the Bathtub

My daughter is knee-diving
in the bathtub.

From the linoleum into
the tub she jumps—is airborne
until she splashes in bubbles and water.

The older she gets, the more I worry
about her banging her head on the porcelain.
The older she gets, the higher she goes.

To be honest, what I'd like to do is
mix a vodka tonic to calm my nerves,
but I won't.

I will sit again on the edge of the toilet,
reminding her not to splash too much—not to pour water
down the air vent next to the tub—not to

jump too high.
The bathroom, our lagoon,
will continue to overflow.

Watch, Daddy, watch!
I'm jumping in, like a sack of feed!

ThIS iS A HOLDUp

A guy with a mullet lights a Camel no filter,
while 200 of you, CEO, vice presidents and customers
stand across the street from the bank.
You have been evacuated.
Someone smelled gas.
The fire trucks arrive.

*Our wing had Mexican for lunch, hope that didn't cause
this stir,* a lady next to you says.

The marquee above the bank
is spitting out NASDAQ figures and
sports scores.
The Steelers are going to Super Bowl XL.

Then it dawns on you.
This is brilliant.
Someone is holding up the bank.
Move to the edge of the curb to get a better look.

Watch a black SUV with tinted windows roll up.
Here it goes.
No one gets out.

*Shitfire! I can feel it.
This is a hold up!*
You always wanted to say that.

A lady on her cell phone turns and
gives you a dirty look.

Police arrive on the scene.
They casually check the surroundings.
Through the big glass windows there's
movement inside—those must be the robbers.
The black SUV isn't budging.

Then it hits you.
Smell of gas—urinal sewage.
Your head begins to ache.

A lady yells, *You can't walk out there!*
Look, look at that fool, she's yapping.
Idiot's going to get arrested.

Here's the gun in your pocket
going off in the air. POW!
You escorting the loudmouth lady,
the gun to her back,
pushing her headfirst into a getaway car,
kicking the door shut—pacing back and forth
in front of the crowd—waving the six-shooter
for good measure to keep the rest at bay.

BAM! BAM! BAM! Fire it hard into the sky.

Anyone else want to come along for the ride?

Ghost on 3rd

At dusk, with my grandpa Cecil
and his soothsayer fishing buddy Russ,
I am on all fours
hunting crawlers.

They hold flashlights
and PBR's
as, with my tweezer-fingers,
I wait to attack.

Don't let go, Junior, one says. *That's a keeper, all right.*
I follow the light beams—back and forth,
back and forth—attack, squeeze and pull
until the night crawler gives
or splits in two.

*   *   *

Grandpa, it's twenty-five years later
and I'm half a world away.
You, skinny as hospital tissue,
lying in a nursing home bed.
Me, on my knees crawling in garden rows
searching for crawlers—engulfed in dirt,
bull snake and mosquitoes.

The last time we fished
I had to ask for help
to lift you from the boat onto the dock,
bluegills and bass gone to grass carp
the size of Harleys.

This will never end, though.
I will take the girls.
I will tell them about the fishhook in my mother's head.
How I saved you from not jumping overboard—
how we hammered fish for years.

Sleep, Grandpa, sleep.
You are the ghost on third
and I'm sending you
home.

The Grass Alley

is just beyond my backyard and I share it
with my neighbors. On morning walks
they creep out of their lilac

bushes. Mrs. McCann, dressed in a light raincoat
and fishnet bonnet,
stops to smell spring

bloom. As she leans in
for a burst of the flower's spell,
she is startled—a dog growl—garter

snake. Slowly she turns
and is on her way. Suddenly
she stops again—

moves towards my overgrown
Pocahontas and Beauty of Moscow,
bows her head and

inhales. What I wouldn't do
when I'm Mrs. McCann's age—
still stopping

to breathe the pleasure
of another new
dawn.

It's My Birthday

It's my wife's birthday and she's pregnant.
She's crying. She's only thirty-four. She's a knockout.

It's your birthday, I say. *You can't cry on your birthday.*

It's my birthday and I'll cry if I want to.

I start in on my own rendition of Lesley Gore's
teen queen hit.

It's my party, and I'll cry if I want to,
cry if I want to, cry if I want to.
You would cry too if it happened to you....

She doesn't find me amusing.
She says I just don't understand.

My wife wants a party, she doesn't want a party.
She doesn't want the mess I've promised to clean up.
She wants peach pie. Maybe chocolate.

Where's the damn chocolate in this house?

If I die and you marry another woman
make sure she's a good mother. You hear me?

A Pony for Paige

Paige, you are only four weeks old
and your sister demands she help out.
I hope you know how proud
she is wiping dry skin she calls *crumbs*
from your face, proclaiming to paint another
red, white and black design you can stare at.

Before that, though, your mother
puts the finishing touches on the barn
she has built in the living room
to house the ponies—blackie Morgan, brown Spirit and
white Joe.
I reinforce the support beams, but can't
for the life of me figure out how to
secure the ladder to the loft.

Some people might think it odd,
a barn in the living room—let them think
whatever they like.
The creatures awake early here.
Willow galloping with colts, fillies and foal
across wood floors.
Your eyes open ever so slowly
to peek at this parade of wild animals.

In between rides
and morning breakfast
Willow checks, then checks again,
to see if you are awake. When she
finds your eyes open
she cannot contain herself: *Look Daddy,
Paige is smiling!*

Then back to the mustangs she trots,
taming first one, then another,
waiting as only a child can wait
for the time when
they can do the tending, tugging
and pulling
together.

Waking to San Quentin

> *San Quentin, you've been livin' hell to me*
> *You've busted me since nineteen sixty three*
> *I've seen 'em come and go and I've seen 'em die*
> *And long ago I stopped askin' why....*
>   —*San Quentin*, Johnny Cash

Pre-dawn
your daughter kicks you
in the chest
as you try to talk her out of nightmare.
Wake the house in thunder.
How are we so easily ensnared
in this space of horror and reality?

Be anxious.
Be nervous.
Triple-check the alarm until dawn.

I.

Stage fright doesn't exist.
Say yes when the Arts ask you to leave your daughters at home
and read for and work with
the hardest of men.

The correction officers will not negotiate for you in a hostage situation.
Hear and understand this. This isn't a game.
Read the contract—black and white.

Think urinal gassings, homemade shanks, newspaper daggers.
Pack your funeral shoes and black boots.
YouTube San Quentin and bypass Johnny Cash—you see, even
the redneck Aryans would've killed for Cash.

You are a skinny little white boy, a colleague says—
they won't leave you unattended.
This trip is nonrefundable. You understand?
Don't forget your lube! The town cop says.

II.

DO NOT WEAR DENIM
OR BLUE TO THE FACILITY
Never allow yourself to be without staff or security.
The DOC does not tolerate sexual harassment—notify authorities immediately.
Do not engage in personal transactions with any inmate. Do not discuss personal
affairs—confine yourself to teaching art. Our program depends on a narrow and
conservative view of our role in the facility.
It is a felony for anyone to assist in an inmate's escape.
Bringing guns, weapons of any kind is prohibited—this includes tear gas, explosives,
and also cocaine, liquor or any other narcotics.

They will try you, immediately. They will see how far they can push—how much you will let

on—how much you will provide. Believe me. I see it every day.

III.

Hop off Sir Frances Drake Boulevard
and just like that you're in their world.
Prime estate in San Fran, the driver says.
Pass through the first armed and guarded entrance after they check the trunk,
into 432 acres that house California's only gas chamber and death row
for condemned inmates.
Park the car in the neighborhood where staff and their families live
(some in trailers they pull behind their pickups).
When a prisoner picks you up in a state vehicle—drives you to the Sally Port,
act like it's all natural—watch him patiently change the dial of the radio.
There you will show ID; be invisibly hand-stamped—as you are
received through three separated and locked
iron gate corridors.

IV.

Do the research. Don't forget it.
Total number of custody and support service staff: 1,718
Annual operating budget $184 million.

Facility Level	Design Capacity	Count
I	215	251
II	1,077	1,564
RC	1,436	2,788
Condemned	554	622
Total	3,317	5,222

Currently there are 33 adult prisons in the state of California. 13 adult community correctional facilities and eight juvenile facilities in California which house more than 165,000 adult offenders and nearly 3,200 juvenile offenders. In addition, there are more than 148,000 adult parolees and 3,800 juvenile parolees supervised by the CDCR.
    —*California Department of Corrections and Rehabilitation CA.GOV*
Hear a man tell you about the problems prisoners face with parole boards—
the Governor's inevitable final say.
Hear him laugh,
kind of—tell you how this place,
demographically, is compared to the country of China.
China.
Hear the echo.
China—a country—get that, man!

*We get the newspaper here. Get a lot of things you probably don't want to know about.
State made chicken coops bigger, on account they weren't humane for a chicken.
Made them cages bigger. We petitioned—did the math—proved our holes aren't large
enough for a Labrador Retriever. Shit I suppose I shouldn't complain—360 guys sleeping
in my room—the gymnasium. Believe that. I can show you, you want.*

V.

Who's house is this?

Our House!

Fear the Mexican Mafia over the three-story barbed and fenced courtyard
doing their hour-long session of strenuous organized calisthenics.
See their shadows—push-ups, deep-knee bends.

Hoo!   Hoo!

Hoo!   Hoo!

You are outside with the pigeons but locked in.
There is a memorial garden for slain officers to your left
and a chapel to your right.
Walk through the courtyard and keep your eyes on.
The convicted men are in blues and t-shirts.

Fresh Fish. Fresh Fish!
A line of new prisoners in their fluorescent orange jumpsuits
 single file—heads slumped—eyes zig-zagging.
Fresh Fish!
Arrive at the entrance of the Prison Arts Program.

*My name is Bird Man. Bird Man, An old gray man says.
Birds like me. Land right on my shoulder.*

It's the truth, another inmate says.

Of course it is. Of course it is. Why he lie about birds.
You see it, right here.

Walk with your group inside.

VI.

You ever have that dream, the one where you
have to choose your ears or your eyes?
Which one would you pick?
Here, we try
to forget both.

Jesus Christ Pose

I walk both sides of this fence.
I have no sympathy for those who premeditate
and execute heinous crimes.

In a theatre practicum in San Quentin
I watch you, a prisoner, standing
in the center of the room.

You raise your hands, palms up,
head dangling down,
your Jesus Christ pose.

You begin to stand on one foot.
The room is quiet. People begin
shifting in their seats.

Minutes pass. You begin to lose your balance.
Every morning, you say, *after my foster father left for work,*
she made me stand in the corner like this.

When your desperate left foot
hits the ground
you scream in the voice of a child

being beaten.
And now I understand why
some of you are here.

I was at San Quentin and All I Got was This Lousy T-shirt

I stand in the Sally Port
to leave the prison and notice one of many signs
hanging on the old stone walls.
Don't forget to buy your San Quentin T-shirt—
TODAY ONLY.

I remember my colleague insisting,
Bring me back a souvenir and don't be
cheap about it.

I'm standing in the parking lot—overlooking
the San Francisco Bay,
inhaling its salty breeze.
This 432 acres is the most desired waterfront property;
even in this bust; lawmakers believe that developers
would pay $2 billion.

I approach the guard—the T-shirt vendor, and like everything here,
it's surreal. There is a line. There are hoodies, various apparel—
all for sale. Proceeds to help sustain
San Quentin's Honor Guard Program.

I buy two identical T-shirts that replicate
a Jack Daniels bottle and that read:

> *San Quentin Prison*
> *Penn No. 1*
> *1852*
> *Cell-brewed*
> *Pruno*

So, I say to the guard, *you're selling T-shirts
that promote a crime within the prison
to raise money for the Honor Guard?*
      Yeah.
Fair enough, I respond, as I turn and enter a vehicle,
driven by an inmate, who will escort us off grounds.
I flash him the T-shirt and ask him
if he wants one.
No way, man!
I'm living this hell.

In a Stall in a College John

and I hear this kid come in, talking loudly,
Hello. Hello.
I think why is there a kid in here?
What kid takes a cell phone
to the bathroom?

Hello. Who are you? Hey? Who are you in there?
I realize then, he's talking to me.
I hunker down on the toilet
like it'll do some good.

I clear my throat. Try to ignore him.
News flashes about a senator
play over in my head—the toe-tapping
hand-jiving closet homosexual—his Minneapolis
bathroom debacle.

What I came here to do is quite simple—you understand.
And, *Hey, in there—who are you? I'm talking to you.*
The kid who won't leave me alone
sticks his hand under the stall.

Don't do that!

Geez, man, I'm just a kid, he says.

I want to tell him; kid, you don't know
what kind of grave you are digging
for me here. If I lecture you like your father should
you will likely leave here bawling.
Where in the hell is your dad?

Geez, man, I'm just a kid, he says again. *You don't have to shout.*

What have we come to?
What forces have swept us in a pile
that used to be reserved for trash?
How is it that we must fear children
instead of love them?
Is it easier to teach fear in everyone?
At what point did the balance
shift for all of us to pay the consequences
for the perverted few?

MISSING

During the 1980s, twenty-year-old John Joubert was convicted of the murders of two boys in Nebraska. He'd gotten his start in Maine at the age of thirteen when he'd stab other children with pencils, razors, and other implements and found that he enjoyed hurting others. He tried strangling a boy and then when he was 18, he killed an eleven-year-old. Then he fled the town. From a broken home, Joubert had been an angry child, and he discovered both solace and power in striking out at others and getting away with it. In Nebraska, he looked for victims while volunteering in a Boy Scout troop. For him, the torture and murder of young boys was a way to relieve sexual tension. But as with all predators, the experience did not ultimately satisfy, so he would soon plan another.
—Katherine Ramsland, *Crime Library*

John, you have been executed—you're
dead. I am thirty-five years old and
I still can't get you out of my head.

I know why I can't—and it's exactly what you wanted.
All the children of Omaha, perhaps
all children, right?
There are theories—stories of you as a Boy Scout leader turned
killer—an Air Force sex ring. A follower.
Perhaps you were kicked like a poor dog
one too many times.

You with your mirrored sunglasses—your hoodie
pulled tight around your head. None of us
will ever forget your police crime sketch
on street poles, milk cartons and store windows.
That Halloween, we went in large groups
and mothers and fathers stayed close behind—some even
with bats—hoping, praying, for redemption.
It was our neighborhood you did this in—
we wanted it back.
How many nights I curled up in a fetal position—staring
at my second-story bedroom window shades
to sleep.
It didn't matter what our parents said,
we invented worry—never again would talk

to strangers—because every one of them
was you.

First grade when I fell on the ice at the bus stop
and an icicle went into my knee—the bus driver
hollering, *Quit your bellyaching—either board or I'm leaving.*
He left and blood oozed as I limped back to the strip mall
in Country Club Village, the apartments where we lived.
A guy came out to help—tried to reach my folks
without luck and took me to school where Mr. Shiver
yanked my arm out of the socket
for catching a ride from someone *you don't even goddamn know—*
that's when I knew my world had changed.

This was the late seventies, peace and love falling;
on the cusp of cocaine—and everyone began living
faster and meaner. This was when you
John, were living with your nightmares, perhaps
calculating rapes, cuttings
and killings.

Ashes, ashes, John—
No
No
No.

Habit

I suppose it's just habit,
when I pass the guys in the yard that I ask,
How's it going?
Always since I was a kid, I'd ask,
How's it going? To strangers—to friends.

Today, as I pass men in their prison-issued khakis
and numbered shirts, one stops and tells me,
Don't you know—you're not supposed to ask us that?
And those few seconds that we stand face to face—
I try to conjure up what I should have said before a guard
orders him away.

What I should have said was,
No, I didn't know. How stupid of me
not to think of something smarter to say.
Me, the teacher, who can leave this prison camp
any time I like.

Vernon is Taking the Dirty Dog Home

On these common grounds, you hope you never
run into each other again. I daydream that maybe I'll spot
some of you. Holding your children's hands—running your tattoo
parlors—catfishing in your favorite holler holes—facing your demons
the best you know how. I think maybe I played a part
in some of this—this, a place any of us could have wound up in
after a few misdirected decisions.

Imagine a greeting from an aging mother who still
relentlessly milks the Holsteins—imprisoned on her own farm,
the smell of rotten silage and the overwhelming burden
of not having enough time. She, though, will be waiting at her threshold,
doors wide open for you.
Imagine the toy brontosaurus on laminate flooring
pointing its head to your child's bedroom—
you will be welcomed again.

When you, Vernon, board that bus to the halfway house
keep your head high. With smart time,
you'll have only two months to go.

I've been instructed never to get too close
to any inmate. But I'm your teacher, and I'm afraid that's just not
possible. Tonight, like most nights,
I carry you home.

The Metal Detector

Through the metal detector
and after the pat-down by police,
we find our seats on hard pews in the courtroom.
We are here to bail out a "friend"
who beat up some innocent bystander—someone who
probably looked at him wrong.

I feel ashamed when I see him handcuffed,
shirt torn from his Friday night brawl.
I am not surprised, though. And I'm disgusted
that I am forking over money for bond.
But I'm still in high school, I'm ignorant
and I don't think for myself.
He stands silently as they read
what he is accused of.
Twice he looks over at us like a pathetic dog.
Just as quickly they take him back into a jail cell.

The judge continues to read off names of the accused—
we cannot leave until he is done.
A 60-year-old man hobbling on a cane is next.
The front of his shirt brown with dried blood—
accused of child molestation.
I want to throw up,
but I can't and I can't leave.

*   *   *

I'm in my daughter's room now.
I have learned to think for myself—to do unto others
as I'd want done to me.

As I tuck her into bed tonight, I wonder:
will monsters with canes
and bloody shirts interrupt what should be
precious thoughts of this world we live in?

I cannot follow her everywhere.
I can only teach her what to look out for,
to repeat over and over,
never to trust strangers—
to think—always to think
hard and for yourself.

Another Poem about the Rain

Two co-eds shoulder to shoulder
stare at the cement—their hoodies pulled tight,
toes curled under—
hen-pecked
walking.

I hate the rain.
    I hate the rain, too.

My backpack is getting soaked.
My sandals are like so spongy.

I wish I had an umbrella.
  Oh, gawd, I wish you had an umbrella.

I hate the fucking rain.
        I hate the fucking rain, too.

The Pecker

Though you always kicked my ass,
you never gave me a black eye.
You threw rocks at my head, but the sting
eventually went away.

Dana Schmitz, you little pecker:
where are you now?

After our last fight
I had to sit next to you on the bus—
the very next day.
I didn't fake being injured.
I was mad that I couldn't beat you,
angry that my puny arms
couldn't throw a decent punch.

On the bus we were assigned seats,
And there's no goddamn way you're switching,
said the driver, who had his reasons.
When I sat down
you made your usual comments.

Listen, I remember saying, *I don't give a care'n hell
if you beat me. The thing is,
I'm not afraid to fight you.
We can go again and again and again.
You don't hit that hard, you pecker.
I can take you.*

His Secret Stash

for Betty Brandenburg
March 10, 1920 - October 19, 2009

After my grandparents moved into my
parents' dining room in Omaha;
after they wound up in South Dakota
one evening after getting the oil
changed in their car;
after the police came and tried to reason
and ask questions about their whereabouts;
we packed their belongings again
and moved them into an assisted living home.

We left my grandfather's rifles and shotguns
underneath the basement stairwell, against his will.
And now, a few years later,
my own parents are moving
and I inherit the guns.

When I look through the cases
a worn black Rolf's wallet falls out.
I know it's my grandfather's although
there is no ID.

Inside are seventeen dollars, three silver dollars;
one for each of his daughters—I'm sure of this,
and an Enderlin Diamond Jubilee token celebrating
the North Dakota town's 75th Anniversary.
The token is good for fifty cents at all
Enderlin banks until July 31st, 1966.

I come to realize that this is his secret stash.
The secret stash he has forgotten about
or misplaced. Or perhaps,
the one that triggered the amnesia,
this disease, this loneliness of memory.

I find his wedding picture
folded and creased five times.
A black and white of my grandmother and him
on the steps of The Little Brown Church.

The pastor is smiling, everyone is smiling.
My grandfather chinless with glee
and my grandmother standing tall, grinning,
her slip exposed.
I try and keep the picture unfolded
as I gently slip it into one of the wallet's plastic
picture sleeves.

All I can do now
is write this.
Should I send it to him?
Should I send it to my mother
to decide?

Makes for 4 Persons

There are secret ingredients in Chinese food;
this is why most Chinese people are slim.
This is my thesis statement and I'm here
to argue.

I want their recipe.
A garlic and ginger
snapdragon mix—the sweet and sour.
Your ancient secret.

I want to eat like a king and be hungry
an hour later—we'll call it metabolism of the
absurd. I want the neighbors to know when I'm cooking—
the scent to run through apartment walls,

like when I was ten, when the neighbor girl Jessica,
who was "dirty knees—look at these"
kissed my mouth and it was all sugar
and spice.

I appreciate your effort, my wife says, *but please,
don't try and make Chinese food ever again.*

Live and learn, I guess.

You always say that, too. Just leave it alone.

*   *   *

Makes for 4 persons,
The back of the sweet and sour soup mix says.
*Crack one egg and stir in one direction for one minute.
Serve instant.*

Do I mix the egg first?
I am making a quadruple batch to feed the Sunday masses
and they are all praying that I don't mess it up;
I beat and put in four eggs.

I realize then, I've blown the show.
Little spit wads of egg float
to the surface. And no matter how long I boil the soup
and add all the necessary ingredients,
it is over. Time to sell the wok.
Time to throw out the Rangoon wraps.
Understand this: a toddler can make Crab Rangoon
and white men can't cook Chinese food.

*   *   *

When I was fifteen
my father's Chinese co-worker
(his family owned a restaurant of their own)
came over for dinner.
Jer-San even brought his mother.
We sat down for a good old-fashioned meal of
pork, mashed potatoes, gravy and, surely,
some corn.
Jer-San's mother kept saying yum yum.
Would shovel some more food and not come up for air.
Then yum yum,
again.
Jer-San laughed. Smiled.
My father, the chef, smiled.
Jer-San said,
American families always try and make us Chinese food.
They should not try.

Poetry Reading—Tonite

The pale poet with his receding hairline;
who is still hanging on to his Pearl Jam
ponytail—who has yet to publish a full-length collection
but has had poems appear in more than
five hundred magazines, journals, anthologies, broadsides and chapbooks,
approaches the podium,
begins tapping on the microphone and speaks.

Hello—hello—is anybody out there?
Syphilis—ssssSyphilis.
The poet sits back down.
Rearranges the stack of journals
he has in his lap.

The mousy woman who says we should wait a few more minutes
to introduce the poet of the hour can't look anyone in the eyes.
She Rises. Sits. Rises and stumbles through the extensive introduction
about the poet's history of lying in biographical blurbs.
His major artistic influence—Mr.
Magoo and trail mix, which keeps him regular.
The crowd of seven move uneasily on steel folding chairs.
Skin peels—an ass suffocates a seat.

I thought I'd start the reading with an epitaph
and then read you a brief essay about the importance
of self-publishing in today's economy—read a few more poems
and then leave some time at the end so you can ask me
questions about my personal life
and my Slamazon.com book reviews.
But before I get to that epitaph
let's hear a poem, shall we?

There are dogs
  There are dog runs—
    The woof woof.
Dripping with hot cheese,
  The waitress winks as she delivers
    The pie to my table.
There are bums
  Who won't get real jobs
    Homeless souls like the I—the I
Who licks himself clean.

The poet scratches his imaginary goatee. Clears his throat
and takes a long drink of the complimentary
bottled water.
Sangria—my fave.
He takes off his reading glasses,
blows hot air on both lenses—adjusts them on his face and asks,
How much time do I have?

Sneaker

I understand the mattress.
The bag of trash.
The *Busch Light* can crushed
on the side of the road—but a
shoe. Whoever: Don't you want it back?

Hopping on one foot in the rain. The stubbed
toe. The hole in an argyle sock.
The flat foot made flatter. Oh Christ!

Every now and again I see that I just missed you—
another of your shoes glistening in the ditch—me pushing on
in this tired crusade.

The Day Before You Broke Your Wrist on the Monkey Bars

You scream at me over the roar of the mower.
You want to ride your bike around the block—
by yourself. Here in this tiny town,
our street that turns to gravel four houses away.
I look up the road and back to you—kill the engine,
tell you not to talk to any strangers
and I swallow hard.

I know this is one small step—one I won't soon forget.
You, Willow, pedaling away—leaning
into the sidewalk's awkward tilt—
training wheels aching to be free.
I cut five rows of fescue—back and forth and pause
to see if I can spot you through houses,
rounding the block.

I think two words; bedrock and believe.
I keep mowing. Soon you appear
pushing your bike through the neighbor's lawn.
You want a drink and to go again, alone.

When I finish the yard and put the mower in the shed
I watch you grab each rung of the monkey bars
without anyone's help. One, two, three, four, five
and a half years old—back and forth, reaching, grabbing
holding yourself in mid-air
without us.

My Five-Year-Old Daughter Questions Death and Spatulas

Do I sound like a bird?
Do flamingos fly?
When am I going to be sixteen?
>*Not for a long time.*

Why does the car have a lawnmower door? Because
 it's funny.

Daddy, did you know grandma's mom
died? How come?
>*She went to heaven with God.*

Did they walk?
>*I'm not sure.*

Am I going to die?
>*Someday honey—but not for*
>*one hundred years.*

Wow! That's a long time.

Why is the fish afraid of computers? Because
it's afraid it might get stuck
in the Internet.
>*You are very smart; you know that?*

Spatulas are the best things ever.
How are spatulas made?
>*I have no idea.*

You want to hold hands and spin around
like this?

Let's look in the mirror and
See how tuff we look.
>*Okay, let's do that.*

Mothers—*A Toast*

Young mothers
it is spring again. Valentines have been sent.
The front doors are ajar—little faces press
against storm door glass.
Put away the disinfectant wipes
and come out, come out.
Fill porches with laughter. Bring your mending
hearts and concerns.
Free those breasts and their veiny road maps
for these little creatures to discover.
And let this be a thank you from all of us
who dart off to work—reluctant to look in our rearview mirrors—
who oftentimes forget to tell you how much
it all really means.

JIM REESE is an Assistant Professor of English; Director of the Great Plains Writers' Tour at Mount Marty College in Yankton, South Dakota; and Editor-in-Chief of *PADDLEFISH*. Reese's poetry and prose have been widely published, most recently in *New York Quarterly, Poetry East, Prairie Schooner, Paterson Literary Review, South Dakota Review, Caduceus, Connecticut Review* and elsewhere. He is also the author of *These Trespasses* (Backwaters Press, 2005, 2006) which includes Pushcart Prize nominated poems. Reese has been the National Endowment for the Arts' Writer in Residence at the Yankton Federal Prison Camp since 2008.

About NYQ Books™

NYQ Books™ was established in 2009 as an imprint of The New York Quarterly Foundation, Inc. Its mission is to augment the *New York Quarterly* poetry magazine by providing an additional venue for poets already published in the magazine. A lifelong dream of NYQ's founding editor, William Packard, NYQ Books™ has been made possible by both growing foundation support and new technology that was not available during William Packard's lifetime. We are proud to present these books to you and hope that you will continue to support The New York Quarterly Foundation, Inc. and our poets and that you will enjoy these other titles from NYQ Books™:

Joanna Crispi	*Soldier in the Grass*
Ira Joe Fisher	*Songs from an Earlier Century*
Ted Jonathan	*Bones and Jokes*
Fred Yannantuono	*A Boilermaker for the Lady*
Sanford Fraser	*Tourist*
Grace Zabriskie	*Poems*

Please visit our website for these and other titles:

www.nyqbooks.org

www.ingramcontent.com/pod-product-compliance
Lightning Source LLC
LaVergne TN
LVHW011429080426
835512LV00005B/338